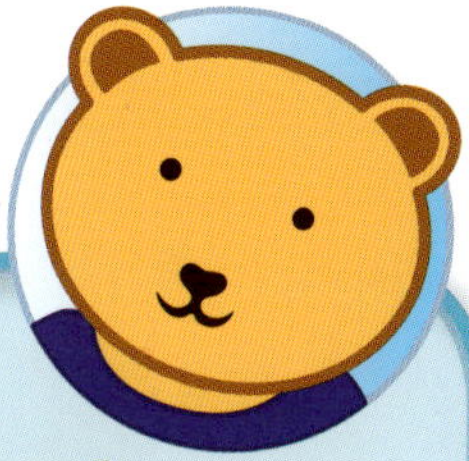

Teddy Horsley Feasts with JESUS

Leslie J. Francis

The Bear facts

Teddy Horsley and Betsy Bear are part of a churchgoing family. They live with Lucy, Walter, and Mr and Mrs Henry. The Teddy Horsley books are designed to build bridges between the young child's day-to-day experiences of the world and major biblical themes and stories. The series is a result of extensive research into the religious development of young children, and the author's wide experience of educational work in schools and churches.

Leslie J. Francis is Director of the Welsh National Centre for Religious Education and Professor of Practical Theology at University of Wales, Bangor.

Published 2006 by CWR, Waverley Abbey House, Waverley Lane, Farnham, Surrey GU9 8EP, England.

Unless otherwise indicated, all Scripture references are from the Good News Bible, copyright © American Bible Society 1966, 1971, 1976, 1992, 1994.

Concept development, editing, design and production by CWR.

Printed in Slovenia by Compass Press.

ISBN-13: 978-1-85345-397-7
ISBN-10: 1-85345-397-8

Other titles featuring Teddy Horsley and Betsy Bear, published by Christian Education, include:

Autumn
Do and Tell
Explorer
Hide and Seek
Lights
Music Makers
Neighbours
Night Time
People Everywhere
The Broken Leg
The Craft Show
The Grumpy Day
The Picnic
The Present
The Rainy Day
The Song
The Walk
The Windy Day
Water

It is Sunday morning and Teddy Horsley is a very excited bear.

On Sunday morning Teddy Horsley gets up early and goes out with Lucy, Walter and Betsy Bear.

Mr and Mrs Henry lead Teddy Horsley past the shops until they come to the church. What will be happening there this week?

Teddy Horsley and Betsy Bear meet with their friends to take part in a play about feasting with Jesus.

Today they choose costumes to become fishermen, shepherds, farmers, bakers, and even Jesus Himself.

The story all began when Jesus took His disciples across the lake to find peace and quiet. He wanted to talk with them alone.

The crowd knew where Jesus was going and rushed round on land to get there first. They were hungry to hear Jesus teach.

When Jesus saw the crowd His heart went out to them. They seemed to Jesus to be like sheep without a shepherd.

Jesus sat down and taught the crowd so many things about God's kingdom, until the sun began to set and tummies began to rumble.

Then a boy brought to Jesus just five loaves and two small fishes. Jesus accepted these gifts with gladness.

Jesus took the bread, gave thanks to God, broke the bread, and shared it around. That day five thousand people were fed.

The story developed when Jesus took His disciples
to the upper room to find peace and quiet. He
wanted to eat the Passover meal with them.

The disciples sat around the Passover table. The sun had already set and tummies had begun to rumble.

Then the disciples brought to Jesus a loaf of bread and a cup of wine. Jesus accepted these gifts with gladness.

Jesus took the bread, gave thanks to God, broke the bread and shared it around. He said, 'My body is given for you.'

Jesus took the cup, gave thanks to God and shared the wine with everyone. He said, 'My blood is shed for you.'

That day the twelve disciples were fed. When the bread was broken and shared they knew that Jesus was with them.

The story continued after Jesus' death when two sad disciples were walking the weary road to Emmaus.

Jesus joined those two disciples on their long journey, but they did not recognise it was Jesus walking with them.

As they walked Jesus taught them so many things about God's kingdom, until the sun began to set and tummies began to rumble.

They arrived in Emmaus and went indoors. Then the disciples brought Jesus a loaf of bread. Jesus accepted their gift with gladness.

Jesus took the bread, gave thanks to God, broke the bread and shared it with them. They ate and their eyes were opened.

That day just two disciples were fed. When the bread was broken and shared they knew that Jesus was with them.

The story continues today all over the world when God's people gather and bring to Jesus a loaf of bread and a cup of wine.

Today Jesus accepts these gifts with gladness. He takes the bread, gives thanks to God, breaks the bread and shares it with God's people.

It is Sunday morning and Teddy Horsley hears
Jesus' call. He knows that when bread is broken
and shared Jesus is there with him.

When Jesus got out of the boat, he saw this large crowd, and his heart was filled with pity for them, because they were like sheep without a shepherd. So he began to teach them many things. When it was getting late, his disciples came to him and said, 'It is already very late, and this is a lonely place. Send the people away, and let them go to the nearby farms and villages in order to buy themselves something to eat.'

'You yourselves give them something to eat,' Jesus answered.

They asked, 'Do you want us to go and spend two hundred silver coins on bread in order to feed them?'

So Jesus asked them, 'How much bread have you got? Go and see.'

When they found out, they told him, 'Five loaves and also two fish.'

Jesus then told his disciples to make all the people divide into groups and sit down on the green grass. So the people sat down in rows, in groups of a hundred and groups of fifty. Then Jesus took the five loaves and the two fish, looked up to heaven, and gave thanks to God. He broke the loaves and gave them to his disciples to distribute to the people. He also divided the two fish among them all. Everyone ate and had enough. Then the disciples took up twelve baskets full of what was left of the bread and the fish. The number of men who were fed was 5,000.

Mark 6:34–44

These questions suggest further ways of developing links between the young child's experience, the story and the Bible passage.

Talk about picnics:
Have you been on a picnic?
Who came with you?
What did you have to eat?

Talk about feeding the five thousand:
Why did Jesus cross the lake?
Who brought food for Jesus?
How much food did he bring?
What did Jesus do?

Talk about the Last Supper:
Who did Jesus take to the upper room?
Who brought food for Jesus?
What did they bring?
What did Jesus do?

Talk about the journey to Emmaus:
Who was travelling to Emmaus?
Who brought food for Jesus?
What did they bring?
What did Jesus do?

Think some more about the story:
Who would you want to be in the play?
When is bread and wine brought to your church?
What happens with the bread and the wine?
What does Jesus do?

National Distributors

UK: (and countries not listed below)
CWR, Waverley Abbey House, Waverley Lane, Farnham, Surrey GU9 8EP.
Tel: (01252) 784700 Outside UK (+44) 1252 784700

AUSTRALIA: CMC Australasia, PO Box 519, Belmont, Victoria 3216.
Tel: (03) 5241 3288 Fax: (03) 5241 3290

CANADA: Cook Communications Ministries, PO Box 98, 55 Woodslee Avenue, Paris, Ontario N3L 3E5.
Tel: 1800 263 2664

GHANA: Challenge Enterprises of Ghana, PO Box 5723, Accra.
Tel: (021) 222437/223249 Fax: (021) 226227

HONG KONG: Cross Communications Ltd, 1/F, 562A Nathan Road, Kowloon.
Tel: 2780 1188 Fax: 2770 6229

INDIA: Crystal Communications, 10-3-18/4/1, East Marredpalli, Secunderabad – 500026,
Andhra Pradesh.
Tel/Fax: (040) 27737145

KENYA: Keswick Books and Gifts Ltd, PO Box 10242, Nairobi.
Tel: (02) 331692/226047 Fax: (02) 728557

MALAYSIA: Salvation Book Centre (M) Sdn Bhd, 23 Jalan SS 2/64, 47300 Petaling Jaya, Selangor.
Tel: (03) 78766411/78766797 Fax: (03) 78757066/78756360

NEW ZEALAND: CMC Australasia, PO Box 36015, Lower Hutt.
Tel: 0800 449 408 Fax: 0800 449 049

NIGERIA: FBFM, Helen Baugh House, 96 St Finbarr's College Road, Akoka, Lagos.
Tel: (01) 7747429/4700218/825775/827264

PHILIPPINES: OMF Literature Inc, 776 Boni Avenue, Mandaluyong City.
Tel: (02) 531 2183 Fax: (02) 531 1960

SINGAPORE: Armour Publishing Pte Ltd, Block 203A Henderson Road,
11–06 Henderson Industrial Park, Singapore 159546.
Tel: 6 276 9976 Fax: 6 276 7564

SOUTH AFRICA: Struik Christian Books, 80 MacKenzie Street, PO Box 1144, Cape Town 8000.
Tel: (021) 462 4360 Fax: (021) 461 3612

SRI LANKA: Christombu Publications (Pvt) Ltd., Bartleet House, 65 Braybrooke Place,
Colombo 2. Tel: (01) 433142/328909

TANZANIA: CLC Christian Book Centre, PO Box 1384, Mkwepu Street, Dar es Salaam.
Tel/Fax: (022) 2119439

USA: Cook Communications Ministries, PO Box 98, 55 Woodslee Avenue, Paris, Ontario N3L 3E5, Canada.
Tel: 1800 263 2664

ZIMBABWE: Word of Life Books (Pvt) Ltd, Christian Media Centre, 8 Aberdeen Road, Avondale,
PO Box A480 Avondale, Harare.
Tel: (04) 333355 or 091301188

For email addresses, visit the CWR website: www.cwr.org.uk
CWR is a registered charity – Number 294387
CWR is a limited company registered in England – Registration Number 1990308

These titles published by **Christian Education**

www.christianeducation.org.uk

A Teddy Horsley Book
The Sunny Morning
Teddy Horsley celebrates the new life of Easter

A Teddy Horsley Book
The Broken Leg
Teddy Horsley meets Jesus in all who help him

A Teddy Horsley Book
The Windy Day
Teddy Horsley and the Holy Spirit

A Teddy Horsley Book
The Present
Betsy Bear meets the Wise Men